Beyond My Dreams

Beyond My Dreams

Copyright © 2015 by Britt Ivy

Published by Silver Torch Publishing
Beverly Hills, CA 90210
www.SilverTorchPublishing.com

ISBN 978-1-942707-22-6

Printed in the United States of America.

Beyond My Dreams

*Benjamin Franklin Ivy III
and Britt Ivy*

SILVER TORCH
PUBLISHING

Beverly Hills, California

CONTENTS

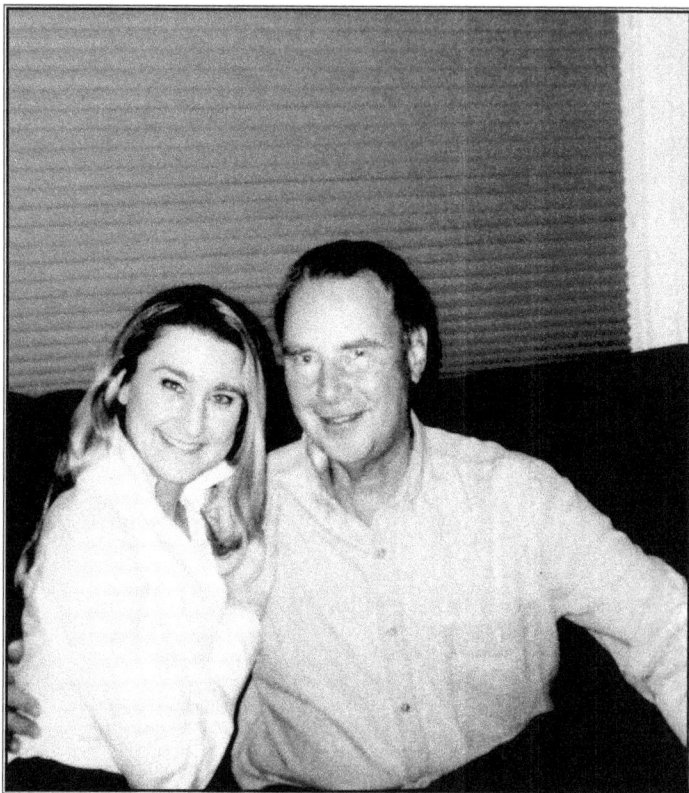

TO DAD WITH LOVE AND RESPECT

Benjamin Franklin Ivy III;
He spoke his truth
Without saying a word
His soul ran so deep
In my heart him I keep

His influence spread infinitely far
He always had his shining star

You're with me now
I don't know how
But 'tis God's gift to me
When you accepted Jesus Christ
I received the comfort
No money can buy;
That you're eternally free.

And when my Lord my soul shall take
At Heaven's Gate You
Wait for me
My dear precious father and our Heavenly Father
I once again will see.

MIRACLES

Miracles begin with the Waking
The singing and buzzing of bees
The sounds of life intertwining
The delight of ideas on the Wing

Miracles begin with the thinking
Awaking the conduit for Man
The Tunnel of all Understanding
The course no one understands.

Miracles are there for the Thinking
The goals that make something of Life
The path for the clear undertakings
The choice as to Diamonds and Furs
The climb to the top of Reality
The singing of songs with the Birds.

The Joys and the Sorrows of Waking
Waiting there, for the Taking, for
Grasping for Miracles
Is no grasp at all.

Britt

Of 16, I have to say
    it <u>must</u> be a glorious day
Of all the things in your life
        I have to say
    your love of people
        makes me so very proud
A doer with real bright eyes
    down to earth,
      definitely – not a child
Definitely lovely, and pure inside
    a true credit to all
        human beings
    not just . . . those who . . . ride!
As time ticks on,
    as lessons are learned
    as jobs are done, and horses shoed,
    as beauty unfolds and fills your
        soul
    as moons come and as moons go
I want you to know . . .
    how special you are
    I love you so

        Love,
          Dad

BRITT

Of 16, I have to say
it <u>must</u> be a glorious day

Of all the things in your life
I have to say
Your love of people
makes me so very proud

A doer with such bright eyes
down to earth
definitely—not a child

Definitely lovely, and pure inside
a true credit to all
human beings
not just . . . those who . . . ride!

As time ticks on,
as lessons are learned
as jobs are done, and horses shoed,

as beauty enfolds and fills your
soul
as moons come and as moons go

I want you to know . . .
how special you are
I love you so.

LION

The lion has a special meaning
Heart full of hope with lots of screaming
He understands our worlds of doubts
As Is obvious within his shouts
Lots of Love does he believe in?
Doubtful though we see it in him
Grandeur synonymous with pain
He shirks not a little rain
Symbolic of so many things, that bring us
out, help spur our game
Ever onward into Fame!
And think, he shirks not, even rain—
for sure knows pain.
May even be a little, just a little, vain.

GRACE

The daily discipline of Love
Brings Grace and Wisdom to Her Being
The gentle Purr of Turtle Doves
The Strength that
Miracles
are made of. . . .
The Knowingness so rare
in Mortals.

The willingness
to WIN.

Britt

My heart sings when I think of you

To think I helped create such a wonderful soul

Soaring over every cliff

I see peace below, not one sharp rift

Sometimes when I view the World

From my perch on high

How simple it is to float, in the sky

The Wind my friend

And the Storms my tools

To gather my strength, for I am no fool

From inside (or out?) there comes a powerful surge

The Knowingness a miraculous balm

for my soul.

Benjamin Ajy

BRITT

My heart sings when I think of you
To think I helped create such a wonderful soul
soaring over every cliff
I see peace below, not one sharp rift
Sometimes when I view the world
from my perch on high
How simple it is to float, in the sky
The wind my friend
And the Storms my tools
To gather my strength, for I am no fool
From inside (or not?) there comes a powerful surge
The knowingness a miraculous balm
for my soul.

TIME

The real part of living
has to do with it
The part most mortals are concerned with
does not
A travesty, a waste of waking hours—
to think
and not to be. . . .
among the flowers
yet fleeing thoughts
determine their destiny
Fleeting thoughts among meaningless matter
really,
in real time,
it is but chatter. . . .
to avoid the moments

Here & Now—
To avoid the glee without the sorrow

To believe the worth
of Beings mortal
To Drink the Soul
and be
Immortal, To Grasp the
meaning of "ever after"

To feel a part of
the "what" we're after!
Skies and Sorrows & little sparrows

PEACE

Peace like this
is very rich

A thrill to the bone
It's so very nice
to finally. . . .
come home

Peace like this
Is heaven beheld. . . .
and cherished. . . .
by every cell

Peace like this
may stop the search
the confusion
the strife
That had become such a large part
of my life

Peace like this I can't describe
but revel
in every line
that tries
to make it even more real
than it is

Glory be, I'm finally. . . .
with me!

PASSION

Counting the depths of the unknown seas
Searching for meaning, and the ways to please
Struggling with, and for, the lost soul
Reeking of Paradise, with stirrings of cold

Saddling mountains, delighted to see
Smoldering coals, reminiscent
So hot
Bubbling heat through the saddle and things
Surprise of surprises
The Mountain is me!

Bubbling, and rolling, and gushing
The unmistakable push of the Universe
Precursor of glee
On top of all that
No movement to see

Save meaning, and love
Little bumps to remind us the path is so close
Confusion abounds, but without any reason
For what is, is and what is not, is not.

BRITT

Seeming to Live
With God on the Wing
Mountains of Pleasure
Feasting with Kings
Lapping it Up
Seeing the Spring
Special Moments
So Happy to Sing!

Minks and Diamonds and Furs
Somehow it always
Becomes a blurr, foggy...
Simply not here
A Glimpse to the Special Place
The Pace on the Mountain
That just isn't Her...

Grasping for Horses
That aren't really Real.

Dad

BRITT

Seeming to Live
With God on the Wing
Mountains of Pleasure
Feasting with Kings
Lapping it Up
Seeing the Spring
Special Moments
So Happy to Sing!

Minks and Diamonds and Furs
Somehow it always
Becomes a blur, foggy . . .
Simply not here
A Glimpse to the Special Place
The Place on the Mountain
That Just isn't Her . . .

Grasping for Horses
That aren't really Real.

THE OCEAN

Glorious feelings of life abound
lessons to learn to keep us sound
Reverence for things within our breasts
to help us survive when it is time for the test
The ocean brings with it air that is fresh
after washing each shore and bashing it clean
the answers to questions asked in all lands
lie in the wisdom contained in those sands
Universal truths of pebbles and pearls
Universal Love is washing the shore
Sounds to admire and accept with full Grace
sights to behold and inhale
To see the meaning contained in this tale
of meanings important unless we're to fail
of meanings to prove the frailty of 'purpose'
attention to thoughts which in action—believe
certain answers to nothing
certainly not the sea

answers only to action, that kind of machines
meaningless chatter, drowned out . . .
by the breeze . . .
the reality of being and seeing the trees
living and believing you already have. . . .
the dream.
The dream of reality to provide you with peace . . .
and meaning, and love
within nothing save the sea and the breeze!
and thee!

BEYOND MY DREAMS

Star-light, Star bright
Omnipotent love on high
Sprinkle my Dreams
With some of those Beams
Of Vast Understanding. . . .

September is here!

Sprinkle the stars to mingle the years
Bring me closer to Knowing
Pave the Path with lights and Sounds
Adding Depth Here
—ever after

Meaning beyond my Dreams,
Real,
for all to See
Ironing out the Wrinkles for me not
for I, after all,
Must See

The Star-light comes best
O're Crooked Paths and Dells
Even scraping close to Hell
Only intensifies the Clanging Bell
Heralding the Light,
That is here
For me. . . .
tonight.

LOVE

Love
is a Miracle
born from above

Love the anchor
the trees sprout upon

Love my own
little Dove

Love again and because
they think
and react

And don't know. . . .

Presents to believe,
live,
and throw!

HAPPY BIRTHDAY (18TH)

TO ONE OF THE CUTEST BIRDS ...
ON OUR FAMILY TREE !

SO YOU SEE
    YOU MUST AGREE
THE SILVER STINGRAY
    FULFILS MY PLEA
'THO A BIT TO SMALL
    TO DRIVE WITH GLEE
BUT FOR YOUR THOUGHTS
    AND DREAMS ...
    THEREIN IT SCREAMS !
TO FIND THE GLEE
    THAT WELLS WITHIN
OUR FAMILY TREE !

    LOVE LOVE LOVE LOVE LOVE, DAD

HAPPY BIRTHDAY (18TH)

... To one of the Cutest Birds ...
on our family tree!

So you see
You must agree
the Silver Stingray
fulfills my plea
'tho a bit too small
to drive with Glee
But for your thoughts
and dreams ...
Therein it Screams!
To find the Glee
That Wells Within
Our Family Tree!

THE PERFORMANCE

Roses with two Lips
The Petals Gleam,
One by One. . . .
Dancing so Beautifully
In the Sun

The message so Clear
This is perfection
Unfolding, Stretching
The Spirit so Dear

Just Being Here
That is Enough. . . .
Singing through
The rest of the Stuff

The bountiful Colours
Dipping Deeply into the Void
Singing to, and Holding
Each beautiful immortal Soul

BELFAIR CAFE

Tokens of Whispers
Edges of Laughter
Wisps of Sky
Sounds of Life
squeaking by
Memories tell us
the Meanings
That cannot pass
us by.

DEAR SISTER,
I WISH YOU WERE HERE.
WHEN ARE YOU COMING HOME?
THANK YOU FOR YOUR LETTER.
SYD IS HUNTING DUCKS TO-DAY.
IT HAS STOPPED RAINING.

LOVE FROM
BEN IVY

P.S. I TOLD MY TEACHER THAT MY NAME
IS BEN.

MY SPIRIT

Her Spirit & My Spirit
Played in the Sun

Knowing forever
the battle was won

The dream and reality
melted, as one
Regarding decisions
there only was one

Two Spirits and one Spirit
dancing forever, together
but One. . . .
basking and complete
In the Sun.

The screw ups would be real,
but really not matter
The knowing was all
and complete.

Perfection, personified
simple and pure
Two souls
now
and another
for sure.

CHRISTMAS

The air brings the familiar smells
Complete with Bells
and stirring thoughts

A time for Peace and Love within
To shine o'er all our families,
and friends.

Remember how the glee transcends
the human forms and frailties
The golden tones of Human voices
rising together. . . .

Vibrating so completely, so fully
To bring God home
within our skin.

Britt

Nineteen is a time for being . . .
more than before . . .
lofty-er
smily-er
softer.
smarter

Nineteen is a time
for silly little rhymes
dancing in the street
bubble bath and reading
sunrise, and love

Nineteen is a time, like all times, for
rejoicing
rehearsing
learning
living, and most of all

Nineteen is a time for
doing . . . like all times,

Nineteen is a time!

All My Love Always,
Dad

BRITT

Nineteen is a time for being . . .
more than before . . .
lofty-er
smiley-er
softer.
smarter

Nineteen is a time
for silly little rhymes
dancing in the street
bubble baths and reading
sunrise, and love

Nineteen is a time, like all times, for
rejoicing
rehearsing
learning
living, and most of all

Nineteen is a time for
doing . . . like all times,

Nineteen is a time!

TODAY

When Love Blooms
The air is Soft
Daily Lessons are Easy and Free
Sidelong Glances are Full of Glee

A Simple Pendulum this one Is
So easy to swing out way
In Softer Air
No need to Push, no room for Despair
A Marvelous Invention
This mushy Air
Swinging Away and Loving the Moment
Think, an afterthought, Hardly Noticed.

IVY FINANCIAL SERVICES

Incorporated, an affiliate of

IVY FINANCIAL ENTERPRISES, INCORPORATED

Registered Investment Advisors

BEN F. IVY
President

September 14, 2001

To our Clients and Friends,

Tuesday's tragedy at the World Trade Center in New York and the Pentagon in Washington has stunned and shocked our country and the world. Many of us will have lost family members and friends, and our thoughts, prayers and sympathies go out to those of you directly affected by this loss of life. I know many of you have concerns about what actions, if any, you should take in response to possibly troubled financial markets. While it is too soon for any of us to have all the facts, we felt it important to communicate our perspectives to you as quickly as possible.

I am writing this letter to reassure you about the financial stability of our country, and to tell you what you might expect to occur in the financial markets once they re-open. Events of this magnitude often have worldwide political and economic effects. In the past, market volatility associated with major world events has been relatively short-lived.

Major tragedies such as this are frightening. While most of us have strong feelings about what happened Tuesday, I strongly advise you not to overreact to these events, by making emotional financial decisions in the short term that would adversely affect you in the long run. We strongly believe that the best strategy is to stay the course through what may be a turbulent market period.

What we do know is that our country is strong economically, and that we will recover from this terrible tragedy. Now is the time to reflect on the importance of family and health. As events unfold and the facts become clearer, we can then discuss what strategic adjustments, if any, are appropriate. We will continue to share our thoughts in the weeks and months ahead. In the meantime, treasure each day with those who are special to you.

With Sincere Personal Regards,

Ben F. Ivy

525 University Avenue • Suite 610 • Palo Alto, California 94301
(650) 328-3800 • (650) 328-3802 • (650) 328-8007 Fax
ifsinc@aol.com • CA Ins. License #0341037

Securities transactions offered through Associated Securities Corp.
Member Pacific Exchange, NASD & SIPC
A Registered Broker/Dealer

FREEDOM FAIR

Let Freedom Ring tonight
Let it Soar on High
and Bless those Hearts!

For Love transcends the "Reality"
that keeps us from Life.
Amplifying blessings so near
We Ofttimes forget they're here!

Let Freedom Ring tonight
A state of Mind
Made Passable by Truth
And brought Alive
by forgetting ourselves
And concentrating on the love we are

Let Freedom Ring tonight,
My Love. . . .
Release it to the skies!

NEW BEGINNINGS

Bold steps to New Beginnings
Many Leagues above the Sea
Faith and Hope I Hear them Ringing
Sharing Depths of Worlds unseen

Eyes so bright and gleaming wildly
starting now to feel the Peace
Gently holding new-found Grace
Taking steps her life to face

Music enters from the Heavens
Winging in with Clarity
Bringing finally the Laughter
Finally,
to seal the Way.

TO BRITT

THIS IS TODAY
(YOUR BIRTHDAY ! TOO !)

AND I'M THINKING OF YOU
AND LOVING YOU
AND CARING ABOUT YOU
AND WISHING YOU THE BEST
OF EVERYTHING YOU WANT IN LIFE

AND NO MATTER WHEN .... YOU
READ THIS .... AND I HOPE YOU WILL

THESE THINGS WILL BE TRUE !

LOVE, DAD

TO BRITT

This is today
(Your Birthday! Too!)

And I'm thinking of you
and loving you
and caring about you
and wishing you the best . . .
of everything you want in life

And no matter <u>when</u> . . . you
read this . . . and I hope you will

these things will be true!

I'M O.K.

She says I'm really O.K.
Happiness is around the corner
Only knock and enter
She says she's really O.K.
Happiness is near
All there is to do is turn
and turn away the sneer
Enter the Kingdom
And relax as the Gods
take over.

LIGHTENING UP

—a proposal

Let's brighten this place
instead of glooming it
Let's sprinkle over
a dose of Zoom!

Let's lift our spirits
up with the Flora
And then
Let's mak-a-luv-a
Forever-a-mora!

How about it?

'LIFE' OR 'est'*

God flies on whispers of our Spirit
Born with each new conception
The reality of the experience creating
all matter
The reality of all matter creating all
experience
The vision of Creation
Flying within our Being
The Vision of Life
Guiding our Spirits

*For Werner Erhard
"About two months after I took est with you in January
of 1979, in San Jose, I started to write poetry. I have
written many poems since then, perhaps a hundred or
so. This one is for you."

To You

Determination sets apart
    this woman with the lovely, lovely heart
The path to wisdom
    a bit obscure
The road to freedom
    a part of her
She lifts her eyes unto the sun, and says
    Lord, oh Lord, what have I done? . . .
How do I know the path of life
    will always include my bright eyes?!!
Oh God I pray the love she feels
    will let her see, the side that is real
    that part of me . . . that heals
Within herself the love of life that says . . .
Thank God for me.
    I love you Bree.

        Benjamin

TO YOU

Determination sets apart
this woman with the lovely, lovely heart

The path to wisdom
a bit obscure

The road to freedom
a part of her

She lifts her eyes into the sun, and says
Lord, oh Lord, what have I done? . . .

How do I know the path of life
will always include my bright eyes?!!

Oh God I pray the love she feels
will let her see, the side that's real
that part of me . . . that heals

Within herself the love of life that says . . .

Thank God for me.
I love you Bree.

Dear Karen,

Here's wishing you a belated (by the time you get this) Happy Birthday! I wrote a little something today when I was thinking about you, and I would like to share it with you, for whatever it may be worth.

" This is a message
          from my <u>heart</u>
I want you to know
          that I am excited about
          your search of life

The growth within your being
          seems a part of me...
          I am so happy for you
          Very happy indeed!
                    To see you feel the
                    Earth and things
          To see you move along
The growth is so apparent
          I want to write a song!

To herald all the things you are,
          and those seeking to become...
          the marvelous and wondrous
          gift

I bring my life upon ?
          Silly though it be...
          it was a part of me

To lift this life above the rest
I now do know—
          You are the best!
I love you,

                    Benjamin "

KAREN

This is a message
from my <u>heart</u>
I want you to know
that I am excited about
your search of life
The growth within your being
seems a part of me . . .
I am so happy for you
Very happy indeed!
To see you feel the
Earth and things
To see you move along
The growth is so apparent
I want to write a song!
To behold all the things you are,
and those seeking to become . . .
the marvelous and wondrous
gift
I hang my life upon?

Silly though it be . . .
It was a part of me
To lift this life above the rest
I now do know
You are the best!

PERFECT FIND

When Dames were Pert
and guys were daffy
and mothers worked and Dads did too,
This Beautiful, Perky
little Lassy
Dreamed Hot, and High
and even Lofty.
Told the stories of love and life
Acting proudly
Dancing wildly
Spunk and Vinegar
No stranger Here
A goddess Really. . . .
Let no one forget
Here's one in a million
a treasure sure
A chip from the Heavens
That's surely Her.

A diamond, A gemstone
A perfect cut
A radiant Beauty
But that's only a start . . .
This one is six million
She's really smart!

AIRPLANES

Airplanes are sort of like people. . . .
They fly to keep closeness away
Airplanes are sort of like people. . . .
Although He didn't mean it that way.

Airplanes are sort of like people. . . .
Looking over the world
To scold, looking down upon the grief
Not to believe the reality
That so starkly lies beneath

The magic of flight defies reason
the magic of flight defies shame
the magic of flight is upon us. . . .
though most often, we don't give it a name

Most often we ignore the reason
we would all really rather soar
and not have to get down in it
and not have to score

But we do, like airplanes above us
We do, as far as the sea—we do because

if we do not, dear
we couldn't be—
Nor would we see why airplanes are like people
Nor would we see why
when everything else is, delivered,

It'll be there for us, in the sky
That's why airplanes are like people

That's why the Moon is so right
the Moon is so right to show people
They don't have to settle each night
But rather can live with the answer. . . .
Though not understanding the sight
But rather can live with the answer. . . .
that won't be here, tonight. . . . or even,
in the morning light.

I'll tell you why airplanes are like people,
I'll tell you what He says is right
I'll tell you why airplanes are like people,

I'll tell you because
see, up there,
Everything's right!

Above is where we all belong
Above is, is, as it were. . . .

And without the flight and the Eagle
We'd all be a bunch of Bums!
Not so glad and so happy to be here. . . .
not glad at all,
but rather as some of us have seen them,
Dead, and nothing at all.

Yes, I love my airplanes,
Yes, I love them all. . . . because. . . .
to me, you see, Airplanes are like people
to them, nothing matters at all. . . .
to them, love and life
are above all.

To them we must lift our remembrance
to them, we believe in it all
to them, who are nothing at all.

But above the rest of those souls
who understand none of it all,
The reason airplanes are like people,
like us,
there's no reason at all!
But to stand tall,
and See it all,
closer to Him
who lives within

Britt Any is Now 21

Skipping and Singing is so much fun
Little stars to hang our hat upon
Swinging in the wind
Laughing and Squeezing
Bring up the Burp and she'll come out Swinging
Diapers aren't everything
Little old Ladies, Know how to Love
     without any swaying
Doughnuts & Beer & Smiles with All Faces
Fun that they Don't Find At Macy's
Leaping & breathing & relaxing moments so real
Just for the Experiance
     but I wouldn't steal!
The Lady is here, we know at last
Finding Such Happiness isn't so fast
Feeling the Breezes take all our Emotion
Oceans of Sweat and Fear
Bringing us near to the Sweet Lady Within
Basking, Finally, in Comfortable Skin.
     From the Dad that Loves You More than
     Heaven & Earth — Love Always! Dad

BRITT IVY IS NOW 21

Skipping and Singing is so much fun
Little stars to hang our hat upon
Swinging in the wind
Laughing and Squeezing
Bring up the Burp and she'll come out Swinging
Diapers aren't everything
Little old Ladies, know how to Love
without any swaying

Doughnuts & Beer & Smiles with All Faces
Fun that they Don't Find At Macy's
Leaping & breathing & relaxing moments so real
Just for the Experience
but I wouldn't Steal!

The Lady is here, we know at Last
Finding Such Happiness isn't So fast
Feeling the Breezes take all our Emotion
Oceans of Sweat and Fear
Bringing us near to the Sweet Lady Within
Basking, finally, in Comfortable Skin.

AIRPORT

Flashing eyes beckon to the gut
Talons of strength
mortar for my soul
Leading me to Heaven
on my way through Hell
Lifting just above the weeds
my destiny
to spread those seeds
Light immersing all that's there
Light allowing us to share
Light is certainly inspiring
Able, too, to keep us dying
Not as Blackness shrouds the purpose
"It" is clear, highlights
each surplus
Emphasizing that which "is"
very much, akin to
Skin!

PEOPLE

The message that lives deep within
So simple, and bright, and pure
can teach us the way, a life so full
If we will but let it in

The pureness and glee of babes is there
No doubts within zillions of miles
A smile and pretty gurgle bring
the tone glow and release of Him

Floating along the Milky Way
Drifting in peace forever
The message and way of the Universe
Somehow confusingly trapped in our skin.

SPRING

April is a comin' out
'Mongst Trees + Skys
+ People

April is my life you see
Without the steeple
Without the with
among the living

To Hear + See
the meaning!

To hear + See
& FEEL It.

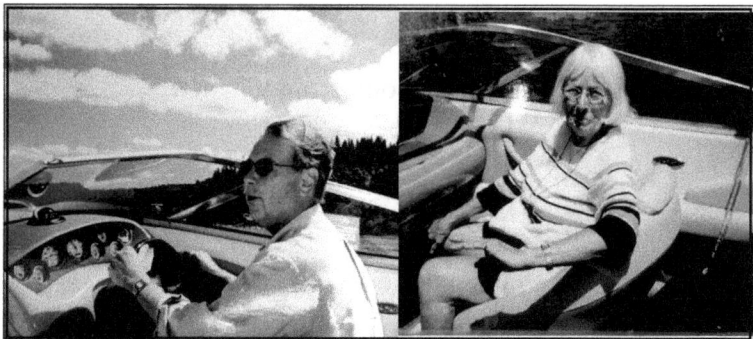

PILLARS

She is the pillar of her life
somehow to cope with the strife
understand the Wind and Waves
a token of the elements she braves

Boats are sturdy, full of curves
it's no wonder they call them 'her'
yielding to each force and yet
somehow, someway staying intact

Not to change a single line
tossed around but still, she's fine
Looking for the land, of course
give her credit—she's not a nurse

Speeding now and then
actually more now than then
still the calmness underlies
to teach her that which cannot be denied
A pillar's strength lies not in the ground
but rather, in something far more sound
molecules within the ship
answer every part of it

Every part of life is there—to touch—
to smell—admire and absorb—
sometimes not so obvious to the wood
of which "she's" built—
my God. . . . she's good!

Flashes of light, and hope. . . .
even though
she's sometimes
misunderstood

Soldiers of fortune mount this lass
and drink it up
from within her glass

Glee could never be described more thoroughly
than to see the world through her eyes
Glee itself could be the book
from whence they came to look it up!

God has words for such fine lasses
thanks to Him I got my seat
listened to the jungle drums
now all I do is sit and hum!

Joy will burst my every seam
I'm glad I'm part of this 'real' dream
While tying up my sailor's knots
I know now I won't sit and rot!

I'll drink you up and spit you out
Go for a ride, then I'll shout
Loveliness hard for this mortal to behold
Will hold me up, preserve my life. . . .
There's no question we'll beat the strife!

MOTION

The poetry of motion
is something to behold
It leaves your life behind you
to appreciate the stars, and think
about the new in life—to feel
the chance to make it right
To feel new blood coursing through old paths,
and renew. . . .
Free the Spirit deep within
and with oxygen and life
To laugh again at things mundane
Their meaning to embrace
To see a new perspective, about
this human (and not so) race
To laugh about the silly-ness
We all put through our paces
To laugh about the way we do. . . .
I don't believe the spaces!
Priorities to look upon, and swallow.

Otherwise, to wallow
Drift as before—probably not even score
If we don't see. . . . the poetry. . . .
of motion
of all else that resides within
The humanness, to be and see
the power that this poetry can bring
If we will only listen!

SOMEDAY

The agony of moments
tortures the very soul
While routines help us hide,
that which we really don't want
to know

The silly-ness of reason
the magic of the unknown
the laughter of the fools we be
won't even let us know. . . .
our soul. . . . and feel the beat of our heart within

That all adds rhythm to it all, somehow
and yet, then, not at all
It adds rhythm, but like routines and
such—masks our very soul. . . .
the reason(s) for our being here
are not for us to know. Or,
are they? No.

The silly-ness of reason, along the road
of life

Is just a way to teach us nothing,
and strife
I've had enough of this, you know
I'll shovel it away!
Someday.
Someday

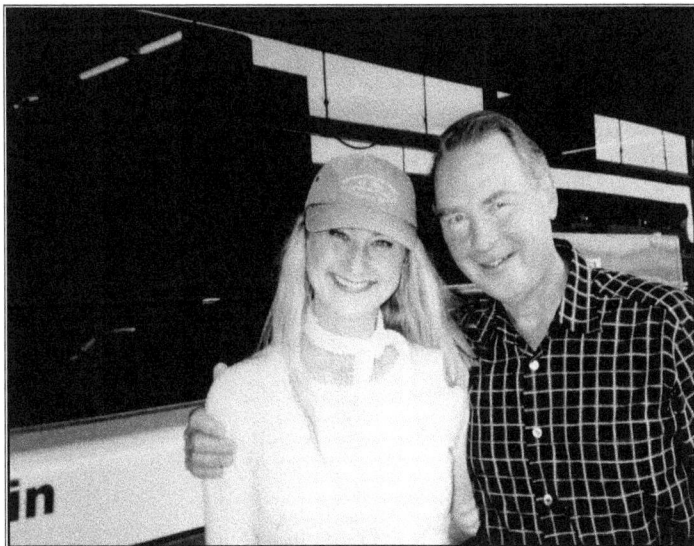

Britta

Her misty eyes were far away
The blinking light she did not see
But filtered sunlight through the ~~to~~ wonder
and big old trees and lots of green
The ~~swaying~~ ponies grazing in the glen
The birds so free, without a word
The smell of musty oats and hay
But peace like this was far away

Then dreams were out, the light was bright
The books still here, ~~but~~ but not so much fright
The calm emerging from deep within
She knew at last her new-found strength

That certain something once buried over
The love of life, unbounded glee
The faith, they say, to be herself
And see the light, sleep through the night
Knowing deeply now
Things will be all right.

Love,
Dad

BRITTA

Her misty eyes were far away
The blinding light she did not see
But filtered sunlight through the branches
and big old trees and lots of green

The ponies grazing in the glen
The birds so free, without a word
The smell of musty oats and hay
But peace like this was far away

The dreams were out, the light was bright
The books still here, but not so much fright
The calm emerging from deep within
She knew at last her new-found strength

That certain something once buried over
The love of life, unbounded glee
The faith, they say, to be herself
And see the light, sleep through the night
Knowing deeply now
Things will be all right.

WELCOME BEN F. IVY

It is a pleasure to announce the appointment of Ben F. Ivy as
an Associate with Mutual Fund Associates, Inc., and Investors
Insurance Associates, Inc., the West's Leading Specialists in
Mutual Funds and Life Insurance.

Ben's office address will be: 3837 Wilshire Boulevard
                                Los Angeles, California
             Telephone: Area Code 213: 385-6237

    As an Associate of Mutual Fund Associates,
Inc., Mr. Ivy's services will be at your
disposal when you seek help with your personal financial and investment planning and
personal insurance protection.

In effect, of course, Mr. Ivy will be Mutual Fund Associates,
Inc., and Investors Insurance Associates, Inc., to the many
of you who have occasion to use our services. Behind him stand
the experience and reputation of our Firms .... their strength
and their reputation in the investment community.

So, on behalf of Ben Ivy, we invite you to become well acquaint-
ed with our facilities. Mr. Ivy looks forward to the opportunity
to serve you who live in the Southern California area.

               Sincerely,

               Harold G. Nahigian,
               Division Manager

HGN/cp

BEN F. IVY

now offers

PERSONAL FINANCI
PLANNING

****

MUTUAL FUNDS

****

LIFE INSURANCE

****

INVESTMENT
PROGRAMMING

****

SECURITY ANALYS

****

THE KIND OF
INSURANCE
INVESTORS BUY

ALIVENESS

Action born of unrecognized motivations
"Shoulds" and "ought to's" to disdain
Sometimes just this side of convention
charm would have to be a name
Little pulses not part of reason, though their
soundness
we can't shout down
Glances, looks, sometimes mischievous
stumbles, falls along with cartwheels
Danger has to be a part here
else the Robots'll come to the 'fore
Or else we may not get out the door
start the journey & it's half completed
share the wisdom of those before
Here with us in all times and seasons
A part of that which we're all here for
common time and common reason
won't let the old newness be a bore
For every tick of the clock brings a newness,

all the same but new once more
New eyes and brains and muscles determine
Those fresh perspectives as we burst out the door
Listening to the scream of reason
Denying it, to "be" once more.

THE SPIRIT

Feelings and Blood, and Bones and Marrow
Sing us songs
Bring us along the road
To realize the motion that resides therein
Encompasses all that we are. . . .
To realize the stillness born of the motion
To allow us to be what we are. . . . pieces of peace to
offer asylum
Dancing, eyes flashing, skirts in a whirl
See what it means
to still be a girl!

Dancing, eyes searching, lurching and leaning
Straining and smiling, we wouldn't be lying?
Water and incense, smells from far places
Help us to believe
We're here, of all places—sighing and feeling. . . .
a bit out of sorts
But lucky to be full of compassion and lust
Lucky to feel it
and see it
Before we are dust!

Lucky in love, it is hard to conceive
Nevertheless it could be. . . .
Playing with the soul and the Spirit
Does not make it less so
But offers its grandeur, the world to enjoy
Shaking, and panting, but filled with the joy of it
Shouting to rooftops—
Release to the white light!
Tensions describe her, oh . . . what a sight
Love & emotion & feelings so proud
Even she knows it, she's glad to be in it
Vital and bouncing. . . .

She's full
of the Spirit

Spirit of Magnificent beings
Spirit that excitement, and brilliance, and beauty
and sound
Will always enhance
and NEVER put down
A land to the sailor,
A ship to the Sea
O Marvelous being
within thee,
I see me.
Flashes of brilliance
Shades of warm trees

Parcels of love to lift the stars
cultivate understanding hearts
long for the answers
that somehow will be
long for the knowledge. . . . that
the beautiful Spirit
Is Free!

HEART'S DELIGHT

Lakes and Mountains, heart's delight
help us to listen to the lights
help us to find the reason sound
our feelings, not . . . to hold down
Seasons to enhance those feelings
that so often,
send us reeling. . . . not to believe
the life within
forcing us
to sometimes, sin.

So what says she with eyes a'smiling
drink up the roses before you're dying!
Grab the mistletoe and run
and while you're at it
Drink up the Sun, smell the wind, feel the
bushes brush your knees
snuggle up to every bough
maybe they can teach you how
maybe. . . . then. . . . but maybe not
When you consider it, that's all we've got!

Lots of maybes, virile branches
Songs to sing and seats to match!
Better move just one more time,
the Sun to appreciate
before the wine.

THIS TIME*

(*or, track.by.track)

Along the Streets of Dreams
The Fairies sat and smiled
Dawdling with their fingers
Pointing, once in a while

Here and there a bauble
a rising of Desire
The strings to which we attach our flies
Or Bees, or whatever comes after

Of pardon and puzzles
The sky is really blue
The clouds, soft and swirl-y,
And clear and Hazy too

Of boys and Violins and Bows
Steamy little Passages
Running along the Streets of Dreams
Slowly eating their Sandwiches
Curly and alive
Come visit, we're Inside.

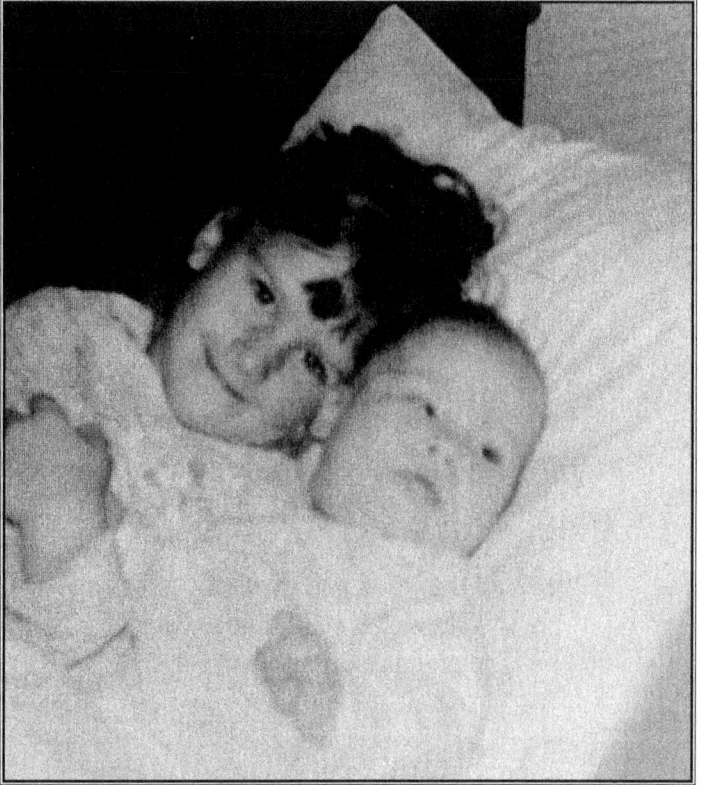

FOR JENNIFER, WITH LOVE

"Sweet Seventeen"

Crossroads and Directions
providing ingredients for life's adventures

Glances and sideways looks
unsettling little thoughts
not to build a life upon

Reality yields the grand distinction
babes in the highchairs
men and women on the mountain

Spirits so real and important and fine
knowing the way of life,
and the why

Leading to the mountain tops, so craggy and wild
singing the songs
that are not very mild

Reality looming
but here the birds
know it all, without any words

Singing in treetops, and down in her soul
gladly accepting
the price of the toil

Knowing the season of light and love
slowly but surely,
ascending like the Doves

Glancing not that mortals do often
digging deeply for the luscious worms
in the backyard

Of life, and of crossroads, we must stand in awe
if we but can see clearly
the plan
In the puzzle.

IT'S ABOUT TIME

Elusive, but what does it mean?
It does not exist
yet holds the key to life
Reality it is not, in fact
it is nothing at all
All causes and things and feelings and
doings
All apples and skies, pigs and molasses
autos and TV and mail
Pass in the night, never found sights
without the circumstance
that holds everything right
A grand illusion, grand to the point
of refuting all reason
rendering useless the topic(s) of
this, or any other, season
Grand and alive, though no life it holds
Grand to be—the substance—of
the soul. The center of life
About which, yesterdays & tomorrows do not reside
So if it isn't, it is illusion
it shouts to present

the beauty
of realism
It does not exist, yet holds everything
A dichotomy of pulses,
without which there is nothing
Understandable only as photographs,
which are, and are not. . . .
Understandable only if we don't try
to understand
Real and unreal
escape it
and we live in strife
Not the heart of life. Accept it, and
flow,
with the unknown
accept it, even though it isn't so.

IMAGES
(from within)

Images of love surge from within
Images of mountains, seas and shores
Images electric to feed out soul
Images that allow us feel so whole

Vibrations that you or I can't explain
teach us we can't take every train
though somehow we know—
someday we'll reach every shore
trying won't help, but we know
We'll do it once more. . . . climb up that slippery glade
stopping too seldom, to bask in the shade

Pale lights of reason, illusions that scream
whispers hard to ignore, no matter—
we know those things don't exist
Our mental images still insist
Listen to us, you are no fool
We're part of you, you learned that in school

Not to forget
the alphabet
Not to tune out
Because he (she) went!
Heaven is never put on hold—Heaven is only
everything told!
Truth as it were, this missive's about.
Truth and to have it, does away with all doubts!

THE SEA

Relaxation pours from every pore
of the breeze along the windswept shore
The sun filters in, every now and again
On top of the smells we adore

The seagulls rise with wings so straight
and swirl slowly into the wind
To turn and alight, so softly from flight
and gaze like the Eagle on high
Six zillion years it took to build
that marvelous spot by the Sea
Unfathomable beauty popping right up
To challenge our thoughts and beliefs

The mystery proud on this day in the sun
Not hidden behind any clouds
But just resting here, so naturally
Inviting us all to come in.

Bird Thoughts, by Ben

Soaring above the Silvery Sea
The thought was So Perfect
                    Why, wasn't it me?

The Puzzle so Puzzling
When lifted so high
                    Can Soar in the Heavens
                    That answers the Whys

Discovering Smiley the Bird Nest of Reason
The long lonesome road
                    That leads back through the Seasons

The twilight of dawning
The Dawn of the light
                    The insights that rest upon
                    The silence of Night

So birds go and come
With omnipotent ease
                    And that's why I love it
                    Up there, in the Trees.

            Written for Britt

                    BD

100

BIRD THOUGHTS

Soaring above the Silvery Sea
The thought was So Perfect
Why wasn't it me?

The Puzzle so Puzzling
When lifted so high
Can Soar in the Heavens
That answers the Whys

Discovering finally the Bird Nest of Reason
The long lonesome road
That leads back through the Seasons

The twilight of dawning
The Dawn of the light
The insights that rest upon
The silence of Night

So birds go and come
With omnipotent ease
And that's why I love it
Up there, in the trees.

PEARLDROPS

Pearl drops of ice form to explain
Lessons to learn with our brains
Windows fog up when it's not very nice
People still do it
Enjoy every night
People will wonder, fight for the sun
always to sing in the light
smiles are more ready
Hope does abound
Believe in the Dream
without any sound?
Pictures of sunshine, pictures of people
Pictures we're after
lifting spirits to the fore
without them it's clear, our Dream is not more

Still photographs & those moving along
All will add meaning
to otherwise blank songs
Real or imagined, it doesn't matter
but without them it's simply. . . .
meaningless. . . .chatter. . . .

Beauteous senses tear down this bold lie? But with
the pictures
we can all reach the sky!

All hold the tones
so clear + so crisp,
in our minds' eye we feel them more dear,
Help us to treasure them year after year.
Droplets of dew giving substance
to souls
Pounding & Dripping and then laying down. . . .
Eager to get to the sky
once again.
Eager to bring us another proud Hen.

WESTWIND

Above the ocean sings a Dove
Sending clearly sounds of Love
Clouds of Doubt cause the others
to Shout
Shut her up, She's not sincere
It's only a Plot to keep us here

She doesn't care, way up there
Doesn't really understand the Burden
We must dig and shove and sprinkle
She has no right to simply Twinkle

If only Doves could learn to sweat
Hustle up the Grits
Sling Hash and worthwhile things
If only they would deal with reality
It's so stupid—
they only sing!
Nothing worthwhile, let's clip their wings!

Stupidity so bold as that, has no place here
where work is King,
"reality"—
and all that "matters."

THE CAT

Swilling full of
Nothingness
Gleaming, rustling breezes
Cares behind or upstairs
Maybe down
Little glimpses of the clown
Nothing threatens
One so sound
Ever closer to the ground
Soothes
and even soother still
Here he is to laugh at you
Beckoning with such bright lies
Labels not existing
Pebbles though—he's had a few
Warm—
Not glistening in the Morning Dew
Near the food & near the table
This Man's life is but a Fable

Lifting up a little here
Scratching sometimes
without a thought
How could all this
Be for naught?

WELCOME TO PARADISE!

Welcome to Paradise
where Birds Fly Higher
Fish Swim Deeper
And Smiles are Brighter!

Happiness Abounds
Invades each Soul
Captures the Essence
Ideality, Complete

A Repast for Renewing
The Hard-Felt Beliefs
That Heaven is Here
Among the Living!

Love me now
Forever More
After that,
I'll Meet you at the Store.

TIME AND I

TIME AND I WE'RE PARTNERS NOW
EYES FORWARD AND ERECT
THE DREAMS SO REAL I SMELL AND FEEL
THE SWEETNESS OF THE CHASE

TIME AND I WE'RE PARTNERS STILL
ALL FEARS OF LOSS ARE ON THE SILL
THE MUSIC PULLS ME UP THE HILL
THE VIEW A REAL EXPLOSION

TIME AND I LIFT UP OUR EYES
A BOLD NEW VISION FORMING
THE PICTURE WORTH THE TOIL AND STRIFE
TO SATISFY OUR LONGING

TIME AND I GO HAND IN HAND
THE WORLD TO SEE, AND THEN EXPAND
THE GLORY CALLING FORTH OUR SOUL
ITS TRUE, YOU KNOW, WE'RE ONLY 25 YEARS OLD!

TO MY DAUGHTER BRITT

Love, Dad

TIME AND I

Time and I we're partners now
Eyes forward and erect
The dreams so real I smell and feel
The sweetness of the chase

Time and I we're partners still
All fears of loss are on the sill
The music pulls me up the hill
The view a real explosion

Time and I lift up our eyes
A bold new vision forming
The picture worth the toil and strife
To satisfy our longing

Time and I go hand in hand
The world to see, and then expand
The glory calling forth our soul
It's true, you know, we're only 25 years old!

WESTWARD AT POINT LOBOS
(Allan Grove)

Life bounding off the Heavens
Shimmering across the Sea
Countless jets of sunlight
Bringing warmth and Depth to the Grove

The magnificence so overwhelming
It's hard to remember to breathe
The people, like colorful ants
come a-swimming
To gaze at the bountiful sea

The earth and the trees so attractive
Seals calling from rocks far away
The perpetual motion of the Universe
captured here, for all time, for all of us to see.

CLOUDS

The shimmering Sun
Incredibly free
Bouncing on top
And underneath me

Lifting me Up
Readying the Surprise
concealing no longer
The reality inside

The Gift of the Moment
Relaxing, and Real
Seeming to Burst
Whatever I Feel. . . .
Leading me Onward
On top of Emotion
The slippery Beauty
Transcending the Oceans,
Inside of me.
Pleasing my Palate
and Me.

<u>Dear Mom</u>

Thank you for the love that sparkled from your eyes
Almost always on the bright side...
Your infectious spirit soaring...
Almost squealing with delight!
I remember giggles, and laughter, and
the unquestioning, unwavering love
nurturing my soul,
and the souls of all those you touched...
Lifting them up
giving them cookies and such
You really were too much!
Just joy and love,
<u>that's</u> what you were made of
Simple really, and <u>alive</u>
A source of great pride! I love you, Mom.

Thank you.   Your Loving Son,

                                    Ben

                                    In Memorium

116

DEAR MOM

Thank you for the love that sparkled from your eyes
Almost always on the bright side . . .
You infectious spirit soaring . . .
Almost squealing with delight!
I remember giggles, and laughter, and
the unquestioning, unwavering love
nurturing my soul,
and the souls of all those you touched . . .
Lifting them up
giving them cookies and such
You really were too much!
Just joy and love.
that's what you were made of
Simple really, and alive
A source of great pride! I love you, Mom.

Eighty Five is quite a while
   Stones to turn around,
   and over
Blue skies and Blue seas
   Reflecting upon
   those dreams
A life of dreams, and honesty...
   Broken pictures now only
   a small part
Pragmatic, and Open, and Loving
   mellow perhaps now...
      Perhaps not!
Perspective, I'd say
   a more noble way
   to say it
Noble enough to call Spades Spades
   and never ashamed
   to show it
Many upon many have known this man
   seldom to find one...
   that doesn't know it!
A statement it seems
   Worthy of those dreams
A statement of Love everlasting!

I love you Syd!

FOR SYD

Eighty Five is quite a while
Stones to turn around,
and over
Blue skies and Blue seas
Reflecting upon
those dreams
A life of dreams, and <u>honesty</u> . . .
Broken pictures now only
a small part
Pragmatic, and Open, and Loving
mellow perhaps now . . .
Perhaps not!
Perspective, I'd say
a more noble way
to say it
Noble enough to call Spades Spades
and never ashamed
to show it

Many upon many have known this man
seldom to find one . . .
that doesn't know it!
A statement it seems
Worthy of those dreams
A statement of Love everlasting!

TO US'UNS

They swim upstream
to be
We

And laugh and cry
a mile up in the sky

Little moments
that swallow our soul(s):
that make us
what we are,

today,
together,
one.

A beauty hard to beat. . . .
this 'un.

THE QUESTIONS

The questions are the answers
From here to yonder shore
Those glimpses help us understand
The reasons we want more

We slip inside the cup of life
And drink, and float along
Then raise our heart to heaven
And ask HIM to sing along

If we believed our billing
We'd swing among the trees
we'd lighten up our burden
And gather honey with the bees

We'd grasp, and open-hearted
Squiggle toes amid the sand
Our Uncle would be something else
If he'd let us join the band

The possibilities abound on high
The pizza pie of life
How we'd swing amidst the daisies
If we could only shake the strife

The daisies have the answers
The questions squirm and sway

Their significance
is lost upon
The grandeur of the bay

Thus thinking is the pond of life
Deep and murky here and there
The grand illusion we behold
As Nature's key and chain

Our efforts are so puny
Let's celebrate and listen
And be among the doe and fawn
And the brilliant grandeur of the dawn

Let's set our sail for where we're at
Let's take a lesson from the cat
Let's squiggle toes amongst the sand
And love the answers here at hand!

THE LOVERS

The young lovers laugh on top of the hill
Eyes glistening in the Sun
The Surf. . . . is alive with the fun
The Angels on high are sprinkling their dust

The stillness of the moment a testimony
Indelibly etched in the stone

The breeze a reminder of freedom so deep
Unspoken, and known of the loved
The setting so perfect,
astonished with the clarity
Their gazes entwined for all time

WHITE EAGLE

Eagles Soar
Searching, leaning toward tomorrow
Far, Far past the shore
Away from Civilization. . . .
where people are no more. . . .

The Sky so blue
Clear and Clean
Beyond Reality. . . .
Fit for Kings
and little people
who've take to Wings

Families of Mankind
So whole and so Free
My People, My Lovers
Who Listen to Me!

EXPRESSION

The creation of our beings
Day by Day
Weaving the fabric
of Joy

The knowingness of each moment
providing the backdrop
the blank canvas upon which
we paint our lives

a daily testimony to the Power
that moment brings
Multiplied to infinity
by the Depth of the Intention
carried within the love
of our beings

Providing the support
and commitment
of which greatness is born.
Day by Day.

A testimony to the Power
of Partnership
Where freedom to be
is the core.

THANKSGIVING

Thank you for the swimming lessons;
Thank you for my beautiful horse.
Thank you for making me a list of chores;
and thank you for paying me and for completing them.
Thank you for food and clothing all those years,
growing up in the beautiful suburb of Palo Alto.
Thank you for the opportunity to attend the finest public
schools;
and for putting me through college.
Thank you for the Honda Accord I received in high
school.
And thank you for telling me the Golden Rule.

Thank you for doing exercises in the morning with me
when I was small;
And playing ping-pong for hours by the pool.
Thank you for the family vacations,
and summer camp at Four-Winds-Westward Ho.
Thank you for letting me help paint Grandpa Syd's
boat;
and serving on the crew.
Thank you for telling me "I appreciate you."

Thank you for talking when I'm feeling down;
And for having fun when we clown around.
Thank you for the countless dollars;
And gifts too numerous to count.
Thank you for your time;
Which is priceless.

Thank you for feeding me for so many years,
and for letting me bring you breakfast in bed so many
years ago.
Thank you for my new Toyota,
and gas, oil and filter.
Thank you for helping me get my dream car Porsche,
and thank you for my Franklin Fund accounts.
Thank you! Thank you! Thank you!!!

Just in case you ever doubt how acutely aware I am,
of all you've done for me over the past 30 years . . .
Doubt no more.
I appreciate you daily in my thoughts,
not often expressed.
Something moved me today,
and whispered to me,
it is time to let you know how much
I APPRECIATE YOU.

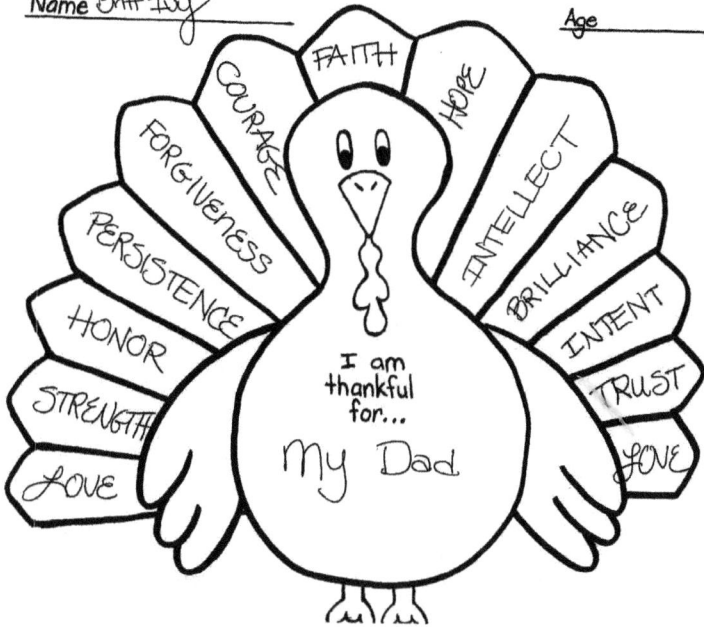

Name Britt Ivy   Age

FAITH
HOPE
COURAGE
FORGIVENESS
INTELLECT
PERSISTENCE
BRILLIANCE
HONOR
INTENT
STRENGTH
TRUST
LOVE
LOVE

I am thankful for...
My Dad

LABELS AND LOLLIPOPS

Swinging toward the fervent sea
Startled, longing to be free
Rising up to meet a Star
Often wondering who we really are. . . .

Fondling each and every leaf
Smelling all the posies
Tripping across the fields and streams
Riding every Pony. . . .

Youth is little and much like that
Roller skates and ice cream
To nearly fit in that well won trip
Had to be a part of the dream

But each and every breath of air
brings newness to the position
The little girls and boys can't know
Such strange and glorious innovations

What thought that thought can improve. . . .

MY LIFE

I've become enamored lately
with the poetry in my soul
To teach me things once only part of dreams
To trip the light fantastic
and whisper in your ear

To live these days in agony
the torture all too real
How can mortals say of this thing, poetry
it helps me move along
I think I must be crazy
to listen to this song
It's not my nature really,
or is it? I don't know.

To dance within the webs of dreams
that are torturing my soul
On top of this I'll be one day
and look askance? . . . . and
laugh! What foolish things these be
my love
Indeed! All's past

The poetry within me
Has struck my life at last
The poetry within me
Has struck my life at last!

Tenseness &
love & bows and arrows
Rafts to float our dreams upon

Not to notice
the size
of the Pond!
All encompasses those who reason
All is, indeed,
in this fine season.
Recognition not a part
the only thing, is her fine
HEART!
The only thing that dopes allow it, is this fine word,
and what's about it! TIME is
all, we must obey—TIME is why we
all must Pray!
That is why illusion abounds.
Everyone is listening for the sounds. . . .
Yet I tell you,
(listen asshole!)
Now! . . . is what we all are after!
Now the minister does reason, now, by
God—and we need no season!

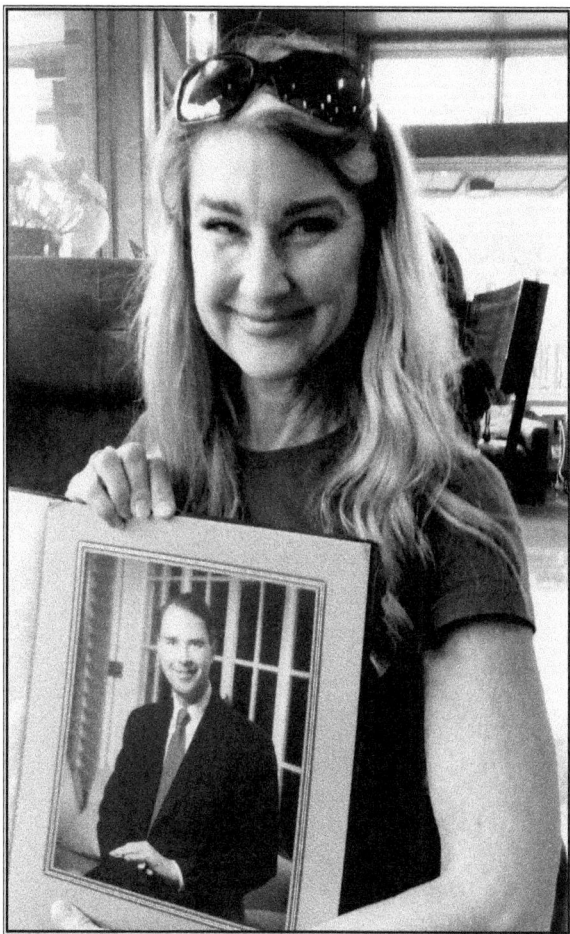

My Meditation

On wings of breath
    Soar mighty Angels
That we might see the Way
Calming evermore,
    the worries of our Soul
Stilling silly yearnings
    Adding depth to those
    still waters ...
Giving support, and running so deep.
    (written for Britt Ivy
      12-24-84)
      BZ

WISHING
YOU,
BRITT ANNEMARIE,
THE MOST WONDERFUL
CHRISTMAS EVER!

YOU HAVE THE MOST WONDERFUL
SPIRIT TO ENJOY
THE MOST WONDERFUL CHRISTMAS!

THANK YOU FOR BEING YOU,
SPIRIT AND ALL —
    I'M VERY PROUD ...

    LOVE,
    Dad
    12-24-84

He who clings to petty contentment cannot possibly attain great joy.

MY MEDITATION

On wings of breath
Soar mighty Angels

That we might see the Way

Calming evermore,
the worries of our Soul

Stilling silly yearnings
Adding depth to those
still waters . . .

Giving support, and running so deep.

About the Author

Benjamin Franklin Ivy III of Palo Alto, California was one of America's leading investment advisors. Traveling often for business purposes, Ben began writing philosophical missives on paper coasters and airline napkins while flying around the world on business trips. "What's a flight if I don't write?"

More than a collection of poetry, Ben Ivy's verses demonstrate the power generated by a gleeful, sometimes mischievous view of life coupled with positive assessments of everyday situations and experiences. As described by the musical term *lietmotif*, there is a recurring theme running through most of the free-form poetry contained in this volume. This melodious thought process answers Professor Albert Einstein's question, "Is the Universe friendly?" with a resounding Yes!

www.ingramcontent.com/pod-product-compliance
Lightning Source LLC
Chambersburg PA
CBHW072013040426
42447CB00009B/1617